An Overcomer's
Guide to Living Well

Dr. Vivian M. Jackson

Cooke, Sam. (1964). "A Change Is Gonna Come". Hollywood, CA: RCA Studios.

An Overcomer's Guide to Living Well
Copyright © 2016 by Harry R. Jackson Jr. Enterprises, Inc.

ISBN: 9781624290909

Printed in the United States of America

This book is dedicated in memory of Essie Rountree Jackson, my mother-in-law. She supported my marriage through the darkest hours of the journey. No request was ever viewed as an imposition. She loved me to the end.

Preface

In the beginning, God created the heavens and the earth...and me. We all begin somewhere. Jesus became the beginning. Because He did, we all can.

I open the book with the story, The Wonder of Christmas. The coming of the Christ Child was a game changer for humankind. God the Father extended an opportunity for all interested people to know Him. Receiving the Christ Child is an opportunity for everyone to investigate. If you love adventure; you will love the journey.

I have never lost a love for celebrating Christmas. I love the Bible stories, the carols, the food, the family gatherings, and the various cultural celebrations. I've celebrated Christmas in three countries on two continents and in warm and frigid weather. Two commonalities in all the celebrations were the emphasis on Jesus' birth and intergenerational family celebrations.

The subsequent short stories find their origin in a seed of truth from my life; observations, struggles, weaknesses, and funny occurrences.

Enjoy a look into my soul.

Foreword

Enclosed are inspiring collections of writings based on the personal journal of a powerful, yet humble, woman of God. By allowing us glimpses into her quiet time, Vivian Michele encourages us to join her in the quest for fulfillment and destiny. These writings reveal how God inspires her to press forward daily, both in the supernatural demonstrations of grace as a pastor and teacher and in the mundane tasks that fill all of our lives. As you meditate upon these entries and embrace the scriptures that ground them, your personal times with God will be recharged and you will be inspired to Godly action.

Marcille Moss and Janice Sherman 2004

The Wonder of Christmas

I could hardly believe my eyes. My breath clouded the department store window as I pressed my face against the glass and strained to see the life-sized figures of the display. The dazzling lights, the beautiful colors, the halting movements of automated animals and people; everything seemed so real. The Sunday school teacher spoke of a baby in swaddling clothes and three kings who came to worship. Right before my eyes knelt the kings and the baby was there in the manger. I wondered what it had been like to travel by camel. Would it be like riding the trolley that stopped on the corner near the department store?

I was aroused from the daydream by the gentle tug of my Nana's hand and slowly walked to the next window. The sight of the big fat guy with the fluffy white hair and beard with toys strewn around the floor connected the dots from the eavesdroppings on the big kid's whispers about how the toys arrived under the Christmas tree. I was looking at Santa Claus! He was the toy connection.

I was conflicted. The guy in the red suit, the worshiping kings, and the little baby seemed incongruent. By kindergarten, I had examined our chimney from the yard, looked into the flue of the fireplace, and concluded that a person larger than me could hardly enter or exit the chimney. I immediately lost interest in the option of Santa!

But I loved to hear the picturesque Christmas story read aloud from Luke's gospel. I listened and drifted into reverie trying to connect the dots and relate to the story. I mouthed portions of the passages as they were read aloud night after night at bedtime.

With my imagination engaged, I made the nightly pilgrimage with Mary and Joseph. I was as surprised as the shepherds at the sight of the angelic visitors and wondered how an angel sounded when he spoke. I marveled that two random old people were hanging out at the church the day Mary and Joseph arrived to dedicate Jesus. I thought it was really fantastic that the old people were in touch with what God was doing and hoped I would be cool when I got old.

As I grew older, child-like wonder matured into awe and a deeper understanding of the miracles of Christmas dawned on me. I saw it; the power of the Immaculate Conception, the beauty of the lofty praise of Mary's Magnificat, and Isaiah's prophesies about the Messiah (Is. 9:6, The Holy Writ). I continued to grow in grace and the knowledge of Jesus Christ and I made the connection between baby Jesus and Jesus the Savior and eventually became Christian.

As a mother, I read the same story from Luke to my children. When reading, I would become animated as I read. Their wide eyes reflecting the innocence of wonder, they seemed to hang onto every word. The announcing angels, the donkey ride, the baby in the manger, the angels in the clear night sky, the shepherds worshiping at the manger and the three kings who visited later. I tried to help them connect the dots from the manger to the empty grave and resurrection of Jesus.

Now I often sit and muse. How wonderful it was to learn that Jesus came to the world as a child, lived in a family, and grew to manhood. His parents trained him and he understood his assignment on the earth (Luke 2:49, The Holy Writ). He fulfilled His assignment as Savior of the world. The precious message of the Gospel is shared annually in the Christmas story and in the carols sung.

The wonder of Christmas is shared in the symbolism of the celebration. The festive decorations of the various cultural groups adorn hearth and home around the world. The lights remind us of the bright star that shone over the birthplace and the stars that filled the clear night sky as the angelic host burst on the scene to herald Jesus' arrival. Evergreens remind us of eternal life that Jesus secured for us in exchange for His spotless life, His death and resurrection (John 3:16, The Holy Writ). Red reminds us that without the shedding of blood, sin is never forgiven (Hebrews 9:22, The Holy Writ). White reminds us of holiness and the spotless life Jesus lived (Isaiah 53:1-12, The Holy Writ).

Christmas *is* the most wonder filled time of the year. Gifts are given and love is shared. But the true wonder of the holy day remains the awe inspired in the hearts of people who connect the dots surrounding the life of Jesus from the cradle to the empty grave and resurrection; who reminisce about their personal acknowledgment of Jesus' purpose in the earth to bring eternal life to those who believe in Him.

Celebrate Christmas with all the gusto and fanfare you have. Lift your voices in faith as the carols ring out. Share your love with others in gift giving and enjoying the holy day meals. Share the Christmas story in your best animated reading voice with the children in your family.

God of Wonders
Psalm 119:68a

Lord, You are good. What You do is good. You are always inspiring us to greatness. I experience such exhilaration when exploring new arenas or learning new concepts at Your direction. You are awe-inspiring, breath-taking, and mind-blowing in the display of Your knowledge, deeds and emotions. I enjoy spending time with You.

~ *Reflections* ~

And Baby Makes Four

What in the world could a baby have to do with the resurrection power of God? The connection between the birth of a child and the resurrection power of God isn't a quantum leap. Both are supernatural experiences.

The birth of a child can be one of the happiest times in life. Other than the first successful experience of mutually satisfying coitus, childbirth ranks pretty high at the top of the list of satisfying life experiences.

Of the many things said about childbirth, I repeatedly hear that pregnancy is a game changer. The article title though somewhat cliché, speaks volumes on the changes involved in receiving a little human into the family. No longer will the two move whimsically along. Planning for three and deferring for the sake of the common good instantly becomes the order of the day.

Generally, women want "to share" the pregnancy experience with their partner. Working to include the partner without nagging and complaining is a possibility. Remember, your partner is not a mind reader. Guess what? No one knows how you are feeling. Talk about your feelings and the kinds of support you need. Although quite a few movies and sitcoms depict the comedic aspects of pregnancy and first births, your situation is different and you must articulate your needs.

Seeking the Lord regarding the pregnancy should not be an afterthought. Accessing His power, strength, and wisdom opens many avenues to comfort, peace, and joy. The idea of allowing the Holy Spirit to guide and nurture you through the nine-month journey can be ignored due to intellect, family traditions, fears, ignorance, and a mind-set that says, that's the way we always do it! After all, you are just having a baby! Women have been having babies for centuries; it cannot be that serious! Such arrogance robs you of unprecedented Divine intervention.

Jesus prayed in the Garden of Gethsemane, asking for strength, comfort, and peace. To complete his three-and-a-half-year journey of ministry on earth, the next steps involved the cross, the grave, and the resurrection. Jesus completed His assignment. You can complete yours too. Allow the Lord to strengthen and encourage you as the months pass.

Resurrection Sunday was THE game changer. All power and authority for every occasion in life was released to Jesus. He has given us access to this same power and authority. YOU have an opportunity to experience resurrection power in a personal way during the pregnancy. When you cry out, "Fix it, Jesus" or "Help me, Lord" things change, circumstances are adjusted, unprofitable conditions are altered. Bring resurrection power into your relationship in unparalleled proportions. Expect to see God's hand move in your life and marriage and in the life of your child. By the way, you + your spouse + Jesus + the baby = four.

A Growing Commitment
Luke 22

Being committed is synonymous to taking a risk. Peter took a risk by getting out of the boat when Jesus beckoned him to walk on the water (Matthew 14:29, The Holy Writ). When Jesus encouraged him to let down the fishing nets, he took another risk (Luke 5:4, The Holy Writ). If I am going to receive all that God intends for my life, I must give up skepticism, the belief that I have all the answers, and take risks! Lord, I must learn to trust You when faced with risks. You will never leave me to fend for myself. Help me be courageous despite any fear.

~ Reflections ~

He Played the Fool

He was growing fast; all legs. It seemed that each month new slacks were required. By the time he went to middle school he was almost 6' tall. Seating arrangements at school were troublesome. I sat near him in elementary school because I was one of the tallest girls in the class.

It is funny how the hassle of being tall in elementary school suddenly vanishes in middle school. Good old middle school. The time when mean people seem to sprout wings and fly below the radar. Snarky comments, barbed jabs, and humiliating tirades are hidden under fake smiles and syrupy conversations, and the best manners masterfully portrayed for adults.

I've often wondered what happened to the victims of mean people. Do they survive three years of unkindness during one of the most fragile developmental stages in life? Do solutions exist to address the growing number of "mean people" in middle school who grow up to be "mean adults?"

A friend of mine says, "That is a home issue." In part I agree, nothing from nothing leaves nothing! However, parents can train children to be polite, loving, and caring. As the old adage says, "People do what is checked." Parents were encouraged to trust the school, and forsake participation on homework assignments, along with the casual drop by the school to see what's going on was strongly discouraged in the late 1960s. The tide of neglect from a lack of parental participation has turned as schools now reach out for parental involvement. I believe the tide can be turned on the "mean people" syndrome too.

Some children seem to display a Dr. Jekyll and Mr. Hyde personality. If a conversation were to occur between the elementary and middle school teacher, neither of them would believe the discussion was about the same child. Needless to say, in many cases the parents remain in the dark unless law enforcement gets involved.

A story is told of one of my relatives who played the fool. The child was exposed at a school function when his mother introduced herself to an invitingly smiling face of a teacher seen at bus duty. Once the teacher realized who she was, the reception cooled off. Later during a reception, the mother overheard teachers talking about her son's behavior on the school bus.

She hatched a plan to follow the school bus the next day. The normal morning routine went without a hitch. Boy on the school bus, mother in her car following behind avoiding detection. She observed her child out of the seat, head wagging in children's faces, and running up the aisle causing the bus to pull over repeatedly.

By the time the bus pulled up to the school entrance, the mother could hardly get out of her car fast enough. As the child's feet touched the ground the long arm of the mother retrieved him. The child was taken away and the board of education was applied to the seat of knowledge. The mother and child rehearsed "the house rules" as they walked back to the school building. The news of the intervention spread like wildfire among the school staff. After the brief intermission, politeness, gentleness, and sobriety characterized the behavior of the one who had played the fool.

What can be gathered from the story?

1. "Have not to be ignored" expectations for your child's behavior.
2. Do not allow work or other interests to deter you from checking to be sure the expectations for behavior are followed by your child, even at school.
3. Be certain the adults who spend time with your child support your "house rules."
4. Do not be surprised when violations occur. A youngster's heart is filled with foolishness, but physical discipline drives it far from him (Proverbs 22:15).
5. Develop a supportive relationship with the school staff your child attends. Call in well a day or two annually and go to the school to serve the school staff. Food and service are great gifts to give.

My Most Precious Possession
Genesis 1:5b

"...And there was evening and there was morning—the first day." Time originates with God. In this passage He steps out of eternity into time. Getting alone with Him to learn from Him each day is one of the greatest challenges I face. Seven days without prayer, Bible reading or meditation still makes me weak!

There are one hundred sixty-eight hours in a week. Lord, convict me of mindless and unproductive activity. Draw me close. Help me use my time to make Your name famous. Famous because of Your character that is seen in my life. Famous because of the exploits done in Your name. Famous because of the impact my life has on generations to come.

~ Reflections ~

Flexing Your Priorities to Serve Others

Relationships can create interesting scenarios in your life. Some people have life all figured out and can easily give God a few assignments to complete on a good day. Others kind of meander through life and unabashedly get a few things done and are happy at the end of the day. But often putting those two peas in the same pod can make life a living hell without three simple ingredients: a) commitment to each other; b) appreciation of unique qualities; and c) a willingness to sacrifice for one another.

When couples come together both parties deny profusely, that the hidden agenda is not to change their partner into what they want and need. I've heard men and women alike say it, "You wait until get through. They won't know what happen." A woman might say, "By the time I wrap him in my arms, his mind goes blank and it will be over and he will be mine." This sounds like something is going on but acceptance of one another seems to be omitted. I think accepting one another was swapped for fixing one another.

Do you remember the movie, My Big Fat Greek Wedding of the 90s? It was a classic! A young man converts to the Greek Orthodox Faith to get his woman. He endures the ribbing of the brothers, cousins, and eats exotic foods. He literally walked the gauntlet to retrieve his Bride. He was committed to have her to the point he was willing to make sacrifices. There were cultural exchanges of food and religious practices. The values of love for family and having fun together were woven into the dialogue.

Every family member had responsibilities. The Greek Papa was king in his castle and the Greek Mama was queen in her castle. They deferred to one another, discussed matters, and issued proclamations. The parents lived in mutual service to one another and their family, steering the clan to their fullest potential of productivity and service.

The struggle for the young woman was that she had somehow lost sight of the values her family embodied. She was looking for something "different" for her life. The young man assimilated into the family through the courtship, the marriage, and the birth of their first child. The movie ends with a compelling scene of the couple is walking their child to Greek School. The dialogue infers that they developed a way to demonstrate their commitment to each other, show appreciation of unique qualities, and a willingness to sacrifice for one another. Corny? Yes. Plausible? Yes. The young love birds took an opportunity and developed an appreciation for their unique differences.

The article title, Flexing Your Priorities to Serve Others is thought provoking. What have you done today to serve someone allowing them to be their best self or to perform at a higher level of efficiency because you served them allowing their gift to shine. Occasionally, a small adjustment in your priorities is all that is required to lift someone over the top and promote a change in perspective that works wonders for them.

Lord, give me eyes to see areas I can serve others. Give me grace to serve without fanfare. Amen

---

Why Did I Do That?
Matthew 6:1

Being self-righteous does not gain points with God. Neither does doing good deeds to be seen by men. Sorry, God is looking at my motivations. In other words, doing the right thing for the wrong reason serves no purpose; self-aggrandizement and pride are impure motivations. A hypocrite does good deeds and announces it to others to receive kudos. Today, I must think about what motivates my actions.

~ Reflections ~

Tender Moments

The morning started like any other, four different alarm clocks sounded announcing the beginning of each family member's day. Shouts resounded through the kitchen as each announced the appointments of their day just prior to closing the door. My husband reminded me of his annual physical and our early lunch date. Dressed in his favorite short skirt, tights, and tailored jacket, I waved goodbye and closed the door. Glancing at the clock, I decided that the time before our date would be spent best editing a recent assignment.

The time passed quickly but my husband did not called to check in. I busied myself; completed the editing project, attached it to an email, clicked send, and smiled with a sense of accomplishment. Yet the phone did not ring nor did he walk through the door. Now he was two hours late; so much for an early lunch and an afternoon of marital bliss.

The phone finally rang. I was not prepared for what I heard. He began by saying that the annual physical appointment went well. Then he lowered the boom saying, "I'm at the Washington Hospital Center to have a cardiac catheterization." My mind clouded over. I could not process what he was saying. The nonchalance in the delivery of his message caught me off guard but I managed to control my emotions making a joke about heart examinations and Valentine's Day.

We had made plans to enjoy an early lunch to miss the giddy young lovers and the press of the Valentine's Day evening rush for restaurant tables. Now I sat anxiously by the phone waiting to receive a call to update me on my lover's heart condition. A blur of activity surrounded me in the home office. People milled about, I heard the sound of the cars as they whizzed past, my head was in a whir. It was hard to focus. I was definitely distracted. Waves of agita flowed through my stomach. Uncertainty is the best adjective to describe the long wait that Valentine's Day.

Hours passed. I paced the floor until I beat a visible path into the nap of the carpet. Remembering funny occasions in our relationship, I smiled as I paced. I became misty at the remembrance of hard times and tense moments deeming them a waste of precious time. The evening dawned, dusk set in, and suddenly it was dark outside. The phone failed to ring. I stood frozen staring out into the darkness.

The piercing sound of the ringing phone broke the deafening silence. Robot-like I lifted the receiver and spoke quietly. The doctor's voice clearly sounded over the hubbub of hospital noises, "Mrs. Jackson? Your husband is fine. He will be released. You can retrieve him in a couple of hours."

Relief flooded my mind and body. Tragedy often creates an awareness of misaligned priorities.

I grabbed a coat and keys and drove to the hospital. I realized I loved my husband deeply and needed to tell him so more often. I retrieved him, we embraced, and I held him tightly, lingering in his arms.

After Thoughts

Be honest. Tell yourself and your spouse the truth about your health status.

Be kind. Control your emotions as you process unsettling information.

Be loving. Love is an action word. Allow your love to be heard and seen.

Be authentically present in the moment. Be aware of the focal point of each life situation. Often you are not the focal point.

Get Up! Get Your War Clothes On!
Mark 4:1-8

Vivian, you are not always at war, but some battles seem more intense than others. Whether the fighting is intense or you are in "times of peace," meditating on the Word prepares you to fight against the wiles of the enemy and brings your flesh under the subjection of the Holy Spirit. You cannot afford to be ignorant of the enemy's devices. Ponder the specific strategies your enemy uses to defeat you. Flip the script. Use scripture as ammunition and take him out!

~ Reflections ~

Difficult Conversations

Recently, I had an interesting experience. Speaking with a person more than 30 years my junior, I was surprised at the similarities in our vocabularies but challenged by the disparity in the meanings of words as the conversation progressed.

It is not uncommon to hold a conversation with someone only to discover communication barriers due to differences in word usage and meaning. True communication or shall I say effective communication implies a mutual understanding of the words used and an ability to pick up context clues.

I'm not sure how far the conversation had progressed before I detected an irritated tone. You know, that all too familiar shrill tightness that emerges when the awareness of disagreement bleeds through. You know, "Ah" (deep sigh), raised brows, and changes in pupil size. Finally, noting the shift in body posture to a more aggressive stance, I was willing to shout, "You are not "getting it!"

As the conversation continued, I was more aware of my annoyance with the conversation's circuitous path. I wanted to shout, "You are not listening. Shush!" Not wanting to appear as rude, crude, or uncouth, I continued seeking clarity all the while working to keep my tone soft and engaging.

The conversation became an effort in futility. Frustrations were high. Neither of us was understood. Remember, the point of communication is to share information with another in an effort to inform, exchange information, or perhaps convince or persuade to a viewpoint.

Understanding carries the connotation of information exchange resulting in an enhanced familiarity or knowledge of something. After about three minutes of "circling the runway," the tenor of the conversation shifted suddenly. The subtle tensions eased. Pupils softened. Tightness around the mouth eased. Smile lines almost appeared in acknowledgment that a failure to communicate existed.

Remembering counsel from a friend, I heard myself saying, "You know, you are probably right. That is an option."

Consider these questions:

1. Why am I so invested in my opinion?"
2. Why does it matter so much if my opinion is accepted or not?
3. Am I keeping abreast on uses of colloquialisms?
4. Is my goal in communication to exchange information or "to make" others do what I say or accept my opinion?
5. In matters of faith, are the "holy words" defined by the holy books or the generally accepted meanings in society?
6. Does a definitive answer exist on the issue?

Advice for difficult conversations:

1. Muster courage during discussions.
2. Acknowledge differences of opinions may exist.
3. Be honest. Disagree if necessary.
4. Avoid being disagreeable.
5. Express appreciation for differences of opinions, but stand your ground.
6. Stop talking.

Meekness
1 Peter 3:4-5

In this passage we are told to have a meek and quiet spirit, which is of value to God. Meekness is the strength to yield to the control of Another. It implies a willingness to lay down your personal agenda for the will of Another. Your mind, your will and your emotions are completely influenced by Another. In 2 Corinthians 12, Paul talks about being meek and having a sober estimation of himself. In verse 9, the Lord told him, "My grace is sufficient for you, for my power is made perfect in weakness." When I grasp the necessity of depending on the power of the Holy Spirit, I automatically yield.

Lord, help me. Meekness is a virtue that I can only gain by entrusting my life to You.

~ Reflections ~

March Madness

As the snow melted from North East Snow Apocalypse 2016 I embraced the advent of spring, new life, and new prospects are on the horizon. Some think of spring cleaning, while others think of taking a vacation. With the dawning of spring, the tenor of relationships often change too.

About 10 years ago our family had taken an apartment in Washington, DC. The apartment provided easy access to Capitol Hill where my husband was working. I teased him all winter about the couples embracing each other in the elevators each night. I reminded him that the commitment to live with fidelity and integrity was waning across the country. Come spring we would see how these relationships panned out.

Surprisingly we had many opportunities during that period to discuss our relationship status. Over a few days we often talked about the state of our union. We were determined to be sure our relationship did not take on a life of its own. Our commitment to each other had been to build strong to last long. Strong unique personalities always present unique differences to work through.

Here are the rules we try to use:

1. Integrity and fidelity are the sieve that sorts our differences.
2. Be objective. Listen to the head and heart of the speaker.
3. Be courteous. Take frequent breaks if needed to prevent free for all arguments and name calling.
4. Stay current. Unless a previous incident is a relevant example, let the past stay in the past.
5. Be willing to discuss personal goals in light of the corporate goals.
6. Closure on a subject does not mean **agreement. Acknowledge the differences. Develop rules of engagement to keep the difference from becoming a hindrance.**
7. Do not create deal breakers. Ultimatums are divisive.
8. Handle personal peeves and preferences with **Biblical finesse. Galatians 5:22-23; 1 Corinthians 13: 4-8a; Proverbs 15:1; 26:20; Psalm 119:165.**

By the way, the building management issued new key fobs. Young love always spring eternal. We saw some of the same individuals in new couplings as we rode the elevator. Sometimes a side-eyed wink of acknowledgment was given as they clung to each other or a knowing smile. All the while I was thinking, the real March Madness had begun!

Search and Destroy
Colossians 3:5-6

We are commanded to "put to death..." those things that will subtly destroy us. Impure thoughts distract, bring condemnation and push us away from God, particularly in times of despondency or loneliness. Unbridled sexual passion is like a forest fire burning out of control, and only the Holy Spirit can quench that unquenchable fire. He helps me battle the passions of my flesh, guard my heart and carefully choose what enters my life through the auditory and visual channels.

Today, Lord, make me aware of the subtle distractions of my life. I want to begin to search and destroy the distractions that hinder me.

~ Reflections ~

He Loves Me, He Loves Me Not

Can you remember the first time your body responded to the presence of a person you were physically attracted to? Do you remember the physical arousal? How about the emotional excitement? What about the mental distractions as you doodle his or her name without thinking? Do you remember smiling at the very thought of that person?

Interestingly, these seemingly benign reactions could be signals or warning signs to keep one out of harm's way. The reactions that seem innocent could prevent hurt feelings or alleviate the fear of rejection. The reactions are normal; examine them. What did you learn about yourself? What did you learn about the other person?

How can one be certain feelings are reciprocated? Can one be certain the scenario is not a "friend in your head" relationship or that one isn't "leading you on?" Initially, the rightness, wrongness, or the intentions of the suitor are somewhat elusive. In most cases you cannot ascertain levels of sincerity. Integrity and fidelity are character traits that surface as a relationship develops.

What do you look for? How do you know if the person is worthy of your time, attention, and trust?

Along the way there will be behaviors that indicate trustworthiness, faithfulness, and follow through. These enduring qualities last after beauty has faded and the effects of gravity are unveiled.

Do you yearn to discover the good and the bad about the other? Does the "mystique" remain? Does that certain je ne sais quoi continue to attract, allure and intrigue you? Are you so turned on you cannot stay away, but you cannot go away either. Interesting feelings...

Be willing to honestly explore an unfolding relationship. Get involved, get invested, or get out. A healthy relationship cycle might unfold this way:

Attraction. You are drawn to each other, "you have chemistry."

Infatuation. You like each other, you are fond of each other.

Affection. You exchange affection—a wink, a smile, touching, hugs, holding hands, kissing.

Conflict. Disagreement, discussion, argument.

Resolution. Settle disagreement(s) and make up (Green, 1999).

The phases of the relationship cycle are repeated and a stronger relational bond can be built. Skipping phases only stalls relational growth. Passing through the crucible of resolution rather than taking the route of avoidance can yield information about levels of compatibility and coping abilities.

As one becomes more infatuated, grows more passionately attracted, and discovers new areas of conflict, the relationship grows in levels of intimacy—emotional, spiritual, and physical. Healthy conflict resolution versus conflict avoidance helps build a strong relational bond. Generally speaking, after several rotations of the relationship life cycle, the tenor of the relationship can tend to be comfortable and accepting for both parties. However, differing desires can create tension and conflict.

A wise old woman is quoted as saying, "Girl, men don't marry. They mate. You have to help a man find the altar." Do not mix your metaphors. According to The Holy Writ, it is better to marry than to burn with passion (1 Corinthians 7:9).

In a word, dating is a horse of another color. Sometimes the rules are not clear. Uncertainty can shroud the purpose of the relationship along with wavering levels of commitment. Oftentimes such instability creates confusing signals.

Questions to Ask Yourself

1. What guidelines do you have for your **relationships?**
2. Are you willing to play house or hard to get?
3. What is your current relationship status?
4. How much of yourself are you willing to give away in exchange for a *possible* relationship?

Study the Word
2 Timothy 2:15

It is only through studying the Word of God that I know what it says. The results of that study are beneficial everyday. The ability to distinguish between the good deal and the ruse or distinguishing sterling character from a rotten egg is enhanced by the active agency of the Word of God. Wisdom comes by studying the Word. Solomon said in Ecclesiastes 1:9, "What has been will be again, what has been done will be done again; there is nothing new under the sun."

Lord, Your words are the most powerful natural and supernatural weapons; in them, I find the keys to unlock truth and understanding.

~ Reflections ~

10 Suggestions to Build Strong Relationships

Giddiness, goofiness, and gratefulness often fill the air as Valentine's Day approaches. Conversations can take on the tone of demand, expectation, or inquiry. Some voices decry the disappointment of years gone by when the desired token of affection was not shared. Others swoon and giggle speaking in hushed tones of the plans made to celebrate and consummate their love.

Like me, many marvel at the expense incurred on one day of expressions while other days a sharp stick in the eye or a passing animal grunt are the normal prize. A seeming lack of consistency in handling interpersonal relationships seems to be the norm. No amount of workshops, webinars, books, small group gatherings, or group and personal therapy can shift you from the center of your universe.

YOU, Sir and YOU, Ma'am will have to acknowledge that your narcissism has destroyed every chance for a meaningful relationship, that the people you rejected were good people, that your fears created excuses used to justify not taking the relationship to the next level, and finally that you are alone with the same problem the first human experienced—no companionship.

There are many complicating factors that contribute to the inability to sustain healthy relationships. I am by no means making cookie cutter suggestions. On the contrary, the 10 suggestions listed below are a beginning point for individuals currently involved in a relationship or individuals desirous of pursuing a meaningful relationship.

Due to the required levels of self-disclosure, selflessness, deference and service to the other; these suggestions are strongly recommended for individuals in marital or common-law relationships. Casuals relationships where individuals seemingly lack "staying power" or ask "what do I get out of this" can find the suggestions too restrictive or demanding.

Check it out for yourself. By the way, forget the life sized teddy bear, two-pound box of chocolate, and the armful of flowers. I'm sure your friend would be ecstatic if you began with an apology for being such a nitwit (male or female) and without fanfare began to CONSISTENTLY display ONE of the traits outlined below. SMH. JAT

1. Steer clear of pettiness. Be kind to one another (Ephesians 4:32, The Holy Writ).
2. Avoid folly. Listen to understand NOT to respond (Proverbs 18:13, The Holy Writ).
3. Keep an open heart during conflict. Extend unconditional love, forgiveness, and acceptance (Matthew 18:15-22; 1 Corinthians 13:5b, The Holy Writ).

4. Be brave. Tell the truth regardless of the circumstance (Proverbs 10:9, The Holy Writ).

5. Acknowledge the need you have to be touched in a right way. Hug each other often for no reason (Romans 16:16; 2 Corinthians 13:12, The Holy Writ).

6. Calm yourself. Rid yourself of the grimace! Smile when you are stressed out (Proverbs 15:1-2, The Holy Writ).

7. Extend yourself. Ask The Lord to help you be "the friend" your friend needs (1 Corinthians 13:5a, The Holy Writ).

8. Treat your friend the way THEY want to be treated NOT the way YOU THINK they should be treated (Romans 12:9, The Holy Writ).

9. Be generous. Give without manipulation (Luke 6:35, The Holy Writ).

10. Develop a realistic perspective about yourself. Be willing to laugh at yourself (Romans 12:3, The Holy Writ).

Annoyed Again?
Psalm 119:165

"Oops, another roadblock! How will I get out of this? Do You expect me to...? I never thought it would come to this!" A tremendous amount of peace is accessible to me today. I am a lover of His words. Absolutely NOTHING can make me miss a step.

~ Reflections ~

Grieving Is a Process. Take Your Time.

I enjoyed having my mother-in-law living with me the last days of her life. Recently, I looked through the photos of her last days. Flipping through my phone, I recalled the mischievous smile, the feisty comebacks, the pregnant thought provoking moments of silence in discussions, the stories of her childhood and college years that filled our days.

The ER staff and doctors sent her home to die on several occasions. After one of those visits, she queried me about the directive received from the discharge doctor. When I told her that the message was that she was going to die in a couple of weeks, she responded that that the man did not know what he was talking about. God would determine when she would die.

It was interesting to observe her over the course of the next weeks. She was more independent, walking more, taking care of herself, and following through with the physical therapy. She actually lived longer than the medical personnel thought she would.

During the final week I was no longer able to care for her. Her strength ebbed away and life slipped away. She ceased to breathe. I touched her arm and realized what the scripture meant by saying "life is in the blood" (Leviticus 17:11, The Holy Writ). The warmth and response to touch dissipated immediately. Her skin had begun to cool. I began to grieve.

I could hardly believe that death was so sudden. In reality the process was not sudden. I recognized the signs of death but would not allow myself to accept them. I guess I believed that somehow, this time things would be different. As I stood at the bedside, my mind flooded with scriptures on death and dying. I remembered my first conversation with Essie as I sat at her kitchen table. She talked to me about seasons of life, marriage, death and dying, and life after the recent loss of her husband of 29 years.

My mind still reels in disbelief some days, especially every Tuesday. She always visited me on Tuesday. Thanksgiving and Christmas dinners were not the same without her the first year after her death. Despite our festive mood, the "the elephant in the room" that we could not speak of was finally addressed when someone used levity to break the silence. We shared stories, told her jokes, laughed, cried, and rejoiced.

I'm a work in process. There are a lot of issues to work through. I was the primary care giver. I alerted everyone that she died. I turned off the machines and "fixed" her before everyone came into the room. I am processing my feelings of loss. Memories, wow I have so many. I smile, I mist up, I laugh aloud, and I become pensive as I process her proverbs that I still don't get. Putting life into perspective after the death of a loved one is a loving work in progress.

Time is needed to process loss. Job's comforters that tell you to get on with life should be ignored. Only you know the depth of your loss. There are five documented stages of grief:

1. Denial
2. Anger
3. Bargaining
4. Depression
5. Acceptance

These stages or tools are similar to scaffolding used during construction projects, the stages help you understand and identify your feelings. These stages are not linear. Each person moves with **fluidity at their pace. Below are a few resources:**

http://www.webmd.com/palliative-care/journeys-end-active-dying

http://grief.com/the-five-stages-of-grief/

On Grief and Grieving: Finding the Meaning of Grief Through the Five Stages of Loss, by Elisabeth Kubler-Ross and David A. Kessler

Questions and Answers on Death and Dying: A Companion Volume to on Death and Dying Touchstone Edition, by Elisabeth Kubler-Ross

Love Your Friends
John 11:35

As a child it was standard operating procedure to say a blessing prior to consuming a meal. I always chuckled when the verse, "Jesus wept" was recited as a blessing over a meal.

I can relate to the feelings associated with the loss of a loved one. Often crying is an expression of loss; and "the deep sigh of relief" is another expression. Jesus cried silently. Unlike the professional mourner who accompanied Lazarus' funeral procession wailing and raising a tumult, Jesus' shed his tears silently. However, onlookers commented on the love Jesus had for his friend Lazarus. Perhaps the perception was that his tears were genuine. I can hardly surmise. I know that Lazarus and his sisters were hospitable and Jesus enjoyed spending time with them.

No doubt the friendship developed with Lazarus was an outgrowth of Jesus' personal ministry to Mary, the times he taught in Bethany and the occasions of enjoying the family hospitality.

All of us need a good friend. I know I do. Lord, give me a bosom friend; one to share my dearest thoughts, aspirations, and dreams. One who can hear the spirit of what I am saying and not judge the clarity or directness in the delivery of the message. One who loves and accepts me. Amen.

~ Reflections ~

A New Perspective on Cyrus— Respect

The citizens of the United States of American spent eight years observing the overt rejection the decision to elect Barack Hussain Obama to the office of President of the United States (POTUS). Many sat idly as disrespectful commentary by national news reporters called the President by his first name, participated in catty discourses about wardrobe choices of the First Lady of the United States, spoke boldly questioning the music selection of the First Family, and made snide remarks about individuals invited to State Dinners.

1 Timothy 2:2 from The Holy Writ, encourages Christians to pray for the leaders of their nation. The benefit of the prayer is a peaceful and quiet life marked by godliness and dignity. In 2008 on stages across the nation, the Democratic presumptive nominee prophesied change to the American public. Some remained poised for change throughout the historic presidency of the first African American President. Others worked feverishly to undermine and discredit his efforts. Looking back over the eight years of his tenure, I would venture to say that Barack Hussain Obama's presidency signaled a change from the status quo in every sector of society.

Many of the citizens of the Republic forgot that the new is not the old. However, President Obama's supportive clear articulation of issues lying dormant in the public square created firestorms throughout his tenure. Many new things were introduced and some old things were reiterated (Matthew 13:52b, The Holy Writ). Despite the general public's espousal of having embraced multiculturalism some of the new initiatives challenged definitions of a variety of cultural groups. The twisting and misrepresentation of President Obama's words often cast a negative shadow, intimated favoritism for a particular group, and stoked the fires of a few arguments.

All the while President Obama kept his finger on the pulse of the Republic. Academics, business leaders, federal, state, and local government representatives and their staffs, educators, researchers, insurance brokers, and all the citizens of the Republic entered an eight-year discussion on the State of the Union as this segment of the experiment in democracy unfolded. As the media continued presenting speculative commentary 24/7, dialogue among citizens in the public square was informed in the context of their philosophical thought influencers.

The title of the article intimates that respect is due Cyrus. Yes, I am aware of several questions quickly surfacing as you began reading. Who in the world is Cyrus? Why should I respect him or his position? Do you think I care? First, I think you care, as the decisions made for the Republic affect your life and the life of your progeny.

In a nutshell, Cyrus, King of Babylon issued a decree for the rebuilding of a Jerusalem during the period of 538-548 BC (Ezra, The Holy Writ). During this time in history the worship practices defined the citizens of a locale. Cyrus, King of Babylon (a pagan of Persia, present-day Iran) was influenced by the worshipers of Jehovah and financed the initial rebuilding of their temple in Jerusalem.

Acknowledging that the Republic has evolved into a patchwork of religious beliefs expands the conversation. Belief systems inform expectations. Expectations inform thought life, thought life informs attitudes, and attitudes inform behaviors. While God's intention if often to give a nation a leader who can navigate through the variegated fabric of expectations and vocalized opinions, thought leaders often mitigate against the process. Expectations often prevent open dialogue and partnerships with persons of conflicting perspectives. Sometimes although a gift horse is present, the horse gets kicked in the mouth. In such a case, a viable option is neutralized. Who knows the thoughts and intentions of a man's heart besides The Almighty? Yet His intention is often thwarted by the small mindedness of **HIS** citizens residing in the Republic. History and Heaven will record the outcomes of the Presidency of Barak Hussain Obama.

Action Steps from another Vantage Point:

1. When conversing, seek to understand versus being understood allows the other to present a position from a different vantage point. Open your ears and your mind.
2. Affirm the difference and do not attack the person.
3. Discuss the commonalities and politely dissect the differences of opinions.
4. Remember **whose** you are and the authority you have in prayer (Ephesian 6:12; Isaiah 2:2)
5. Push pass the fear of being rejected because your opinion may not flow with the mainstream.
6. Work on recognizing a "gift horse" among us.
7. Take advantage of the gift of national **leadership.**
8. Participate. Register and vote. Your life matters!

Speaking Truth to Power
Acts 26:24-39

Paul, the apostle had an opportunity to speak with Herod Agrippa II. Paul made a compelling appeal for the Gospel telling the story of his conversion. Interestingly, neither Agrippa, brother-in-law Festus, nor Agrippa's sister Bernice, made a decision to receive Christ.

The response of Herod Agrippa II to the Gospel is very telling, "Almost thou persuaded me to be a

Christian..." I wonder how many people are almost persuaded and never decide? I wonder what the deal breaker was for Herod Agrippa II?

Lord, give me words to pray for the leaders governing the nations of the world. Leaders need a source of wisdom that exceeds the intellectual capacity of mere men. Give us world leaders who are wise individuals who respect the I AM, and honor the principles of Scripture. Amen

~ Reflections ~

No, You Cannot Have It All

"My friends, a mist in the pulpit creates a fog in the pews!" My thoughts trailed off as I envisioned the room being filled with fog as the preacher prattled on. As I daydreamed, ever so slowly the preacher faded from view. He was so corny, eliciting laughter as he described disastrous situations where leaders failed to lead. He added a turn of a phrase here and there, lots of mother wit, and practical examples of lessons on leadership principles. Yes, the preacher was corny but he was also wise.

As a learner, I take a posture of reflexive thought as I sit in seminars. I try to "get it" by applying a principle or two to my life in the moment. Why wait? No time like the present to be the best me. How can I use the principle NOW?

I was aware that my personal life was lopsided. I was unclear in the articulation of goals and expectations. Momentum from previous successes swept me along to new venues and exciting learning opportunities.

But the matter of the mist and the fog continued to rumble through my thoughts. I began a conversation with my husband to get the level of clarity I required. My closest friends provided input. Often the bleed through of ministry demands that one minimize the needs or dreams of the family. The tyranny of the urgent devours time and spoils precious moments. My children offered the best input; "just do what you say. No more excuses." Out of the mouth of babes...

Life transitions can assault the senses leaving a leader whirling in uncertainty. A confused leader only leads people into confusion. I had to get brutally honest about likes and dislikes, strengths and weaknesses, and positive and negative relationships. I needed to be clear and concise about my goals. I had to separate myself from the tentacles of ministry to get in touch with ME. We had children to lead.

I asked myself, "If money and opportunity were not barriers and I could do anything I wanted, what would I do? Was further training required? Whose names made the short list of supporters? Who were the accountability partners?

According to leadership guru John Maxwell, everything rises and falls on leadership; I had to face the fact that my family was lost in a fog of my indecision? I was shaken by the realization. Without a destination, any road can take you there! Without vision, people perish!

I often speak of being authentically present in the moment. I checked in with my family to get their perspective. I interviewed each family member to understand his or her needs and expectations. From the conversations, I assigned myself one thing I would work on for each family member to demonstrate my concern and leadership.

As I continued to be concise and sought clarity, peace prevailed in my home. Whenever I allowed personal fears to overwhelm me, I was swallowed in the fog of confusion and indecision. I settled it. My quest for balance in my life put me on a trajectory with laser focus. I asked God for courage to stay the course. Life became less complicated. I gave direction in critical family situations to build stronger relationships. I operated in the principle of rewarding approximations rather than seeking perfection.

The preacher may have been corny, but he really knew what he was talking about. If I am unclear or uncertain, I breed insecurity in those who are walking with me. I pray God will continue to give me grace to lead with boldness each time the baton of leadership is passed to me. And no I cannot have it all. But I can enjoy what I have.

Are Those Reins in Your Hands?
Psalm 119:68b

Teach me Your decrees. Lord, cause me to grasp the full import of Your words. Do not allow me to be a know-it-all. I want to understand the intentions and motivations for Your actions. Draw me close like You did with Moses. Speak to me; give me direction for my life and for those You have called me to lead.

~ *Reflections* ~

Food is Fuel

Hmmm good! Lemon pound cake, chocolate chip cookies, kettle chips, vanilla ice cream and grape soda. I'm in junk food heaven and loving it!

Seriously though, I love freshly baked cookies and pound cake. I eat kettle chips with vanilla ice cream and grape soda. None of these treats have any nutritional value. The sugar rush is phenomenal and hunger follows shortly afterwards.

Empty calories rarely provide the energy necessary to engage in thinking work or expending physical energy. Our bodies are designed to efficiently burn fuel. Eating a proper diet provides the necessary fuel to sustain life.

Being sure to eat protein, vegetables, fruit, the good fats, grains, and complex carbs requires thought, planning, and TIME to cook. I often ask myself, "Do I feel like cooking?" "Do I want to cook today?"

Interestingly, I grew up eating home cooked balanced meals daily. I didn't eat a lot of junk food. I cooked daily when my children were young. Now as an empty nester, I exercise other options.

Discipline is required to make the right choices about food. One thing is certain; no one can make the decision for me. Join me in making wise choices about food. Let's eat the foods required to allow our bodies to function at the optimum level.

Eat a proper diet.
Eat items from all of the food groups.

Remove processed foods from your diet.
If it didn't come out of the ground, spit it out.

Be willing to shop twice weekly for fresh meat, fish, vegetables, and fruit.
Remember, the fish market is closed Sundays; "fresh" fish is unavailable Sundays in most stores.

Skip the aisles displaying sweets and snacks.
If you don't have it, you won't eat it.

Drink half your body weight in ounces of water each day.
You might think you are going to float away, lol.

The Scriptures encourage a balanced perspective in all areas of living. Hold on Vivian. Don't get psyched up and go on a campaign. Be aware of your choices. Be willing to change your mind if a better choice exists. Enjoy your journey.

Symbols of Sacrifice
Leviticus 2

Verse 11 says, "*Every grain offering you bring to the Lord must be made without yeast, for you are not to burn any yeast or honey in an offering made to the Lord by fire.*" Leaven is a symbol of pride, malice and hypocrisy; honey represents sensual pleasures—attributes of the sin nature.

Accepting Christ puts an end to the legal authority of the sin nature in my life (the honey and the leaven). Jesus, influence my choices. I want to be more pleasing to You.

Let these virtues (fruit of the Spirit) of humility, sincerity, peace and purity replace the attributes of my out of control sin nature. Amen.

~ Reflections ~

I Need a Father

Early memories of my life are filled with activity. There were sounds of laughter, music, and sounds of pots and pans banging in the kitchen. The aromas of savory food, butter and sugar from baked goods and the smell of smoke wafting through the air. Layered in the air were the sounds of adult discussing important issues, children giggling, babies crying, and the banging of a screen door.

Significant voices and conversations seemed to always include my grandfather or referenced him in some matter. As the patriarch, his counsel was sought by everyone. Later memories are of routines and significant events. Daily routines of sitting over the heat vent on a red kitchen stool as the warm air filled the room, remembering to take items out of the freezer for the evening meal and changing the loads of clothes from the washer to the dryer.

My family always arrived in shifts in the evening. I was usually the first to arrive, and then my siblings, then my mom, and later other relatives would drop by. The evening routine was about the same each day; the waiting period, meal preparation, homework, cleanup, homework and bedtime.

Meal preparation was undergirded by the sounds of the top R&B songs blaring from the radio. We sang along, danced and talked about the happenings of the day and made plans for the weekend. Conversations continued through the meals and cleanup. We helped each other with homework and prepared for bed. Each day was basically the same.

As a teenager, I became acutely aware that I was missing something. I needed a man to tell me I was competent, smart, and could achieve anything I wanted to do. Being a pretty face with a nice figure and a brain was not enough to satisfy my soul. At that point in my life, most of the men I met were trying to bed me down.

I needed a father. Although I could not articulate my need, what was offered was not what I wanted. I knew I was drawn to strong men. Men who seemed to know what they wanted for life. I wanted a man who possessed character and integrity. I wanted a mentor; a man similar to my grandfather. I wanted a mentor with a great sense of humor, full of wisdom, who was a lifelong learner, and a lover of people.

In my twenties, I was introduced to a few men who were mentors. Each made significant contributions to my life. I am aware that fathers can make five contributions to the lives of their children.

1. Approval—speaking favorably to the child.
2. Acceptance—communicating their ownership

of the child, receiving the child, and expressing gladness that the child is present.

3. Affirmation—being proud of the child, showing appreciation.
4. Affection—showing affection by touching, holding or hugging the child without sexual touching.
5. Authority—setting limits in leisure time **activities, explaining protocols of world systems and modeling appropriate life skills.**

Although I have never met my father, God's plan for my life included those men who filled the voids along with the overarching sense of His love for me. I'm not perfect. I am aware of my needs and can articulate them. I am bold to go after the fulfillment of those needs. My Heavenly Father watches over me.

Contentment
Psalm 119:14

Lord, You have won my affection. I no longer search for other lovers. I am satiated with Your love. I will keep myself for You alone (Exodus 20:1-6, The Holy Writ). Jesus, You are the King of my life and the lover of my soul. May I always find peace, rest and contentment in Your words.

~ Reflections ~

Tell Them I Sent You

As a child, I was often sent on errands. Initially, I was given a note. Once I had proven trustworthy, I was allowed to speak on behalf of the sender. The scenario would go something like this: Directions would be given outlining what I supposed to retrieve or the message I was supposed to deliver. I would be queried on the content of the message to make sure I could repeat the message without changing its content or intention. The final directive was, "Tell them I sent you. Be certain to use my name."

Jesus began His ministry with the end in the mind. After He gathered His posse, He modeled the Kingdom lifestyle. He went about teaching, healing, performing miracles, influencing religious and governmental leaders, affecting social systems, and serving people. The influence of the Gospel literally affected every sector of society (Matthew 28:18-20; Mark 16:15-20; I Peter 2:9, The Holy Writ).

One of the most difficult tasks encountered in life is delivering a message in the name of another. Maintaining the tenor of the message "true" to the tone or texture of the sender is a challenge. Messengers have been ridiculed as parrots or yes men or women, endured physical assault and even death delivering their messages. Yet many messengers forge ahead knowing the critical nature of their tasks.

Think about it. Messengers are needed. How can we increase the number of messengers influencing societies around the world? Should young men and women be enlisted? Is it considered radicalizing or proselytizing to enlist young men and women? At what age should delegated authority be discussed and released to others?

Delegated authority has been given to establish the Kingdom of God in the earth. Will you carry the message? Will you go in His name and influence every sector of society? Consider these principles:

1. Live your life according to the principles outlined in Scripture. (Psalm 111:10; Proverbs 1:7, The Holy Writ)
2. Be willing to look at "your craft" through the lens of Scripture. How do the principles of the Kingdom of God influence your practices?
3. Familiarize yourself with others who influence society as messengers.
4. Ask Jesus to show you in the Scriptures how using His name as a delegated authority can influence society.
5. Join other messengers and multiply your efforts.
6. Strategize with others to access untapped resources.
7. Ask the questions, "What about our progeny? How can I include them?"

8. Develop relationships with others.
9. Allow trust to grow. Trust is based on skill and relationship. Trust is NOT given to strangers.
10. Use the responsibility test to develop skilled messengers. Give feedback.
11. Follow the principles recorded in the life of Jesus. Those who pass the responsibility test can be given delegated authority.
12. Go. Tell them who sent you. Enjoy the journey.

Unlock the Favor of God
Isaiah 65:8-10

God extends mercy to others because of my relationship with Him. Nations are preserved, families are kept safe, and children are rescued. God declares that as His people seek Him, He responds with favor.

Smile, and revel in the understanding of your value in His eyes. Families, companies, even nations can be shielded from destruction because of your presence. Vivian, you are blessed by Him to be a blessing to others.

~ Reflections ~

Leaning on the Everlasting Arm

I remember sitting I church with my legs dangling from the pew looking at the rather wide derriere of the lady standing in front of me. Her bouncing hips keeping time as she played the tambourine. She threw her head back as belted out, "Yes, I'm leaning on Jesus..." My mind wandered as I tried to visualize her leaning on Sunday School Jesus barefoot, sitting on a boulder with people around him. I chuckled as I envisioned her in her starched white dress and white hat with veil in white duty shoes, standing in the sand on the beach with Jesus. It is funny how the imagination paints pictures!

Fast forward to the 21st century and I can still hearing that lady singing her heart out as the rhythmic pounding of the tambourine thunders in my ears. Now here I stand, trying to reassure myself that *I'm leaning on Jesus* and not my own understanding (Proverbs 3:5; 4:23, The Holy Writ). Decisions, choice and opportunities are submitted for His scrutiny. Which way is The Lord leading? How do I know what to do? How can I keep myself from the precipice of disaster?

I struggle with this dilemma. I become **frustrated, often angry, and fearful. Sorting through emotions is challenging because I want to** cut my own path. Sometimes I would rather leave Jesus in the altar, do my own thing, and pick him up on my way back from the adventure. Invariably I yield and look back marveling at the miraculous power of Jesus that keeps me from destroying myself.

What constrains me? What is it that sifts through the bent to sin and iniquity warring within? Sometimes I am aware of God's hand directing me. At other times, I only recognize His help in hindsight. Here are a few principles that guide me.

1. God's counsel to my heart is always correct. I have to mature to hear His voice and silence my evil (condemning) conscience (Hebrews 10:22, The Holy Writ).
2. God's counsel can be confirmed in the mouth of two or three witnesses. Not my boyfriend or girlfriend, but legitimate mature saints who know the ways of God. If I cannot bring the matter to counselors, it is probably foolishness and cannot bear the scrutiny of examination (Matthew 18:16, The Holy Writ).
3. I am selfish and want my way ALL the time. I can easily deceive myself and convenience myself that ANYTHING is the will of God (Jeremiah 17:9, The Holy Writ).
4. I must examine my motives by a Biblical standard. I have to ask myself, "What does the Bible say about the situation?" I must search the scripture for the answer and be willing to

follow the revealed principle (Psalm 119:105, The Holy Writ).

5. I keep telling myself, that if the offer is too good to be true, **it is** too good to be true. In each instance, I have to balance that thought with the principle that every good gift comes from my Heavenly Father. I exercise **discernment and examine the hand on the other side of the opened door of opportunity. What kind of character does the person/organization have who is extending the opportunity? Are they worthy of my trust?**

Yes, I'm leaning on Jesus, Christ my Savior and like you, I struggle to yield. I was young and now I am old, but I reached the same conclusion as in my youth. Old habits die hard. Satan, the accuser of the saints tenaciously declares that he will return to his house (my life) despite having been expelled. I declare, I'm in it to win it! God is the strength of my heart and my portion forever (Psalm 73:26, The Holy Writ). The eternal God is [my] refuge, and underneath are the everlasting arms. He will drive out [my] enemies before [me], saying, 'Destroy them!' (Deuteronomy 33:27, The Holy Writ)

Hoffman, E. A. (1897). Leaning on the Everlasting Arms. Public domain

Honoring God
Nahum 2:13

The people of Nineveh repented when Jonah preached to them, but soon a business as usual attitude set in. They did not receive the words of the prophet Nahum; their hearts hardened. The desire for "creature comforts" took control in their lives. In their unwillingness to return to God, He turned away from them, declaring in verse 13, "I am against you."

Wow, if the Word of God does not saturate my heart, I will be unable to honor God and I will experience the bitterness of His wrath. I must turn to the Lord; He is waiting for my reply. Lord, help me to always answer in the affirmative. I submit my strong will to you. Amen

~ Reflections ~

Finishing Well

Reflection, thanksgiving, celebration, and looking forward should be integral parts to the end of any involvement. The New Year signals new beginnings, pushing the reset button with a few minor changes. Many people begin to evaluate and catalogue the accomplishments of the year of with excitement and gladness. Others become pensive and express feelings of regret over the results of their labor. Both attitudes are legitimate expressions of feelings during a period of reflection.

What makes the difference in the reflexive reactions? I believe the key ingredient is the giving of thanks. Often we forget that an invitation to the Perfect Party was never extended to us. However, an acknowledgment of the sustaining grace and mercy of God, the networking of relationships, unsolicited resources dropping into your lap and the reporting of results that were immeasurably more than you asked or thought are reasons to be thankful.

Celebration is often associated with the giving of thanks. The woman in the parable of the lost coin, exuberantly called her friends to rejoice with her when the coin was found (Luke 15:8-10, The Holy Writ). Occasionally it is necessary to reflect and give thanks with celebration. Many use the phrase, "stop and smell the roses;" I say, "stop and throw a party. Invite friends to mark the goodness of God in your life."

In 2011 I was in the midst of weekly infusions of chemotherapy that made me dreadfully ill, sick to my stomach, and unable to keep food and liquids down. I asked by friends to help me have a party to celebrate life! The party—Elegant Little Black Dress Party has become an annual celebration of life for women in the DMV and the East coast. Now the cancer is in remission, and I am thanking Jesus for His healing grace, and celebrating life daily.

Finishing well implies an assessment of the kindness Jesus and others have extended. Evaluate the good, not so good, bad, and ugly occurrences. Be true to yourself but avoid harshness. Name calling is not permitted. Be as objective as possible. Here are a few questions to support the evaluation process:

1. What did I learn through the experiences?
2. What information can become a part of my swag?
3. How can I protect my thought life to prevent introspection that leads to depression?
4. What steps of action will protect from other negative influences of failure?

Decide to keep a thankful heart. The novelty often associated with success can be accompanied by a sophistication that seeps in along with the desire to excel or be great. The greatest challenge you face while finishing well is remembering that God opened the doors, extended the relationships and opportunities, and provided the resources. He brought you (Deuteronomy 8:10-18, The Holy Writ). Remember to say "thank you" Determine to finish well; you are entering another year of transitions.

A Purpose-Filled Life
Luke 22:39-53

On the Mount of Olives, Jesus came face to face with the purpose for His existence. It was there that He uttered the words, "...yet not my will..." My home, job, with relatives or a circle of friends are avenues He uses to give me a purpose-filled life. Bailing out is not an option.

Today, I will chart a course toward knowing and understanding the will of God for my life. In the process, I will have a deeper relationship with Him. Jesus, help me to recognize Your unfolding purposes for my life.

~ Reflections ~

And the Walls Come Tumbling Down

It is interesting to note that the infrastructure of the Unites States of America is crumbling. Motorways, highways, bridges, sewer systems, the electrical power grid, and rail systems are in need of repair. During hot summer months, population hubs experience power failures as demands for power escalate. Bridges are tumbling down. Pot holes swallow tires. Landslides wash away roads. The water table is low often resulting in restricted use. Hundreds of thousands of gallons of water flood roads as antiquated water pipes burst all over the nation.

These natural occurrences are a signal to the spiritually astute. The subtle demise of the systems that support life and commerce are eroded due to neglect. Costs associated with upkeep have been passed on for the future seemingly with attitudes of nonchalance. Let someone else take care of it. No tax increases on my watch. The mantra NIMBY resounds loudly on bumper sticker and protest placards. Years have passed and it seems the **infrastructure is falling around our ears.**

Poor spiritual lives and personal lives often mirror the demise of the infrastructure of major cities. Lives are overbooked, over committed, and often too busy to be creative and reflexive. The advent of the mobile phone has put a majority of people in an always on state. The tyranny of the rung, buzz, or flash interrupts would be quiet moments into the late night hours. Time once spent conversing, thinking, and getting to know others is swallowed by distractions.

Are the wall of your life and personality crumbling? You can recalibrate your life today. Take an inventory of your life, wealth, and relationships. Consecrate your time, talent and treasure to The Lord. Meditate on the Holy Writ. Get centered and focus on your life's purpose. Decide to use your time to make a difference serving others. Serving others can open opportunities and income streams for you.

Reflect and Move Forward
Isaiah 46:8-10

This passage focuses on the significance of the past. God says in verse 9, "Remember the former things, those of long ago; I am God, and there is no other; I am God, and there is none like me." Looking back at God's performance helps me believe what He has said about the future. Take time to reflect on His faithfulness. Move forward. Go ahead. Just do it!

~ Reflections ~

Standing on Thin Ice

I had hardly closed the door to the office when I looked up to see a flock of mallards. Some were paddling through the frigid water, while others were standing on the frozen pond. It occurred to me that often life's choices were very similar. One could jump in and get involved or stand on the sideline and reject an opportunity.

I noted that the ice seemed rather thin in the section of the pond closest to me. Yet many of the mallards seemed content to stand on the glassy surface surrounded by the jagged edges of melting ice. I stood musing about my life. After five years of catastrophic *illness* I often found myself uncertain in the midst of choices. Once I was always certain, answering quickly with confidence, planning ahead, anticipating the need, often answering correctly before being asked.

Now as the brisk wind whisked across the pond, like the mallards, I tucked my head inside the collar of the scarf and walked away. As the wind beat my face, I looked over my shoulder to see mallards leaving the ice to enter the frigid pond. I asked myself, "Should I take advantage of the opportunity extended or wait? Perhaps I was being premature in considering the option without an official offer. Now may not be the optimum time."

I watched tree branches sway as the wind picked up and suddenly a few of the mallards were flying to another location on the thin ice.

Life really is full of sudden occurrences. Just as the gust of wind suddenly blew across the pond and the mallards took flight, situations can be presented that offer new experiences and opportunities. Nothing in life is certain except taxes and death. Now is the time for me to be certain, to rise in faith, to ride the wings of the wind and come to my desired haven. Standing on thin ice may not be as precarious as it sounds.

Meditation on the Word
Mark 4:1-8

My decision to walk with You is similar to a seed that is planted in good soil. As I decide to live for You each day, I mature and become more Christ-like. When I meditate on the Word of God, it becomes engrained in my mind and takes root in my heart. Meditation denotes thinking deeply about something for protracted seasons, to ponder a scripture, to muse or "daydream." As I memorize scriptures, the words provide the power I need for breaking through in every area of my life. Think about your favorite passage today. Receive strength and guidance.

~ Reflections ~

Overcomer

As I pushed the handle of the door to walk out of the doctor's office that brisk winter afternoon, I knew that I was in for a fight for my life. I took my husband's hand and we walked down the path toward the car. We stopped and embraced. As I rested my head on his chest he said, "We are going to get through this."

I knew the fight had begun, yet numbness filled my soul. The words of the diagnosis rang in my head like the chimes of the cathedral bells of my childhood tolling the time on the quarter hour. Cancer, multiple myeloma, blood cancer, chemotherapy, prolonged anemia, and stem cell transplant. Yet in the back of my mind, I could hear a still small voice echoing, "Jesus Christ the same, yesterday, today and forever." My mind swirled, yet an anchor settled my soul with the comforting thought that somehow Jesus was aware of my situation and would come to my rescue.

In the weeks and months that followed I read about the disease, received prayer for divine healing, and filed paperwork to begin medical treatment. Time seemed to fly as I attended the weekly appointments for chemotherapy, antibiotics, bone marrow biopsies, blood transfusions, and check ins for the complete blood count aka CBC. Peace filled my heart and a positive attitude flooded my mind.

It was not until the day of the stem cell transplant that I acknowledged how sick I really was. Intellectually I grasped the concept of contracting cancer. Intellectually I grasped the fact the Jesus was the only answer for my case. Intellectually I grasped the concept that the stem cell transplant was the best treatment for me.

However, as I laid on the hospital bed, in and out of consciousness, totally unable to care for myself I began to connect the dots. I was hanging between life and death. I was in need of help for real. In the background an IMac played the holy scripture aloud on a continuous loop. Suddenly, I heard passages of scripture rumble through my mind declaring the power of God to heal, to bring victory, to empower, to enlighten, and to cause ME to be an overcomer. I was no longer involved in an intellectual pursuit. I made a connection with the God of the scripture, with Jesus, The Christ, and began to own the promises for my life and wellbeing. I had a blessed assurance.

As the stem cell transplant team entered the room I knew that the power of The Christ was present to prevail. I knew that I would make it through. Using my own stem cells in the transplant, the process lasted 45 minutes, but the healing process took five years. There were days when I thought I would die. Waves of despair flooded my soul. There were numerous trips to the ER because of a crisis. I spent years hooked to an

IV weekly receiving chemotherapy. Nausea, incontinence, vomiting, and dehydration were my constant companions.

Darkness seemed to overwhelm me. But songs of deliverance flooded my soul. I often heard the voice of Holy Spirit singing on the inside and listened to the words of familiar melodies. After several rounds I opened my mouth in agreement and gave voice to the Word of the Lord for my situation. "I am not forgotten, God knows my name..." "Never would have made it without YOU..." "You came to my rescue..." "Encourage yourself in the Lord."

I began to say what God was saying, sing what God was singing, and hum what God was humming. I knew that I would be healed. I knew that I would live and not die and declare the glory of God. My friends, I worked with the grace extended to me from the word of God, the prayers of the saints, the songs of deliverance, the tears I cried, the fears I pushed aside, and I held fast to the precious promises given in scripture about my situation, circumstance, and condition. There is no cure for multiple myeloma. Drugs are used to keep the cancer in check.

Despite the use of a variety of chemotherapies, remission was not achieved until the fifth year. Oh yes, I overcame by the blood of the lamb and the word of my testimony! I recognize that every situation is different, that I made mistakes along the way, but this I know; Jesus is a healer. The path to remission was circuitous; it was neither magic nor instantaneous miracle. I'm still standing. I fight to maintain the victory!

I'd love to hear your testimony of overcoming! Write me at drviv@the-marriage-doctor.com or tweet @marriagedoctor2.

Renewal
Isaiah 40:31

Circumstances, situations and conditions cause me to forget that God is Almighty, that He sees and knows everything and that He has it all under control. It is easy for me to begin to lean toward what I can do and what I know, and rationalize situations based on my intuition and intellectual prowess. Get the playbook (The Holy Writ). My best reasoning is not enough. I need the power of the Holy Spirit and the Word of the Lord in order to soar like an eagle. Vivian, relax. Wait on Him.

~ Reflections ~

I Know My Change Is Gonna Come

The notes of the sultry voice of Sam Cooke continue to resound through time, "I know a change is gonna come, oh yes it will." No matter your age, as a human you have longed for a situation to change. Recently I was forced to face a situation that tried my patience and character. Toiling over how long? When? How? I was faced with the fact that I was unable to force the progression of the desired change.

Looking back on the situation, I realize that the steps of action I took managed the change process. These are the steps I took.

1. Manage your attitude. I removed negative influences from my environment. I was challenged enough by the situation. Negative input would not support the process. I surrounded myself with those who supported me in the change process.
2. Expect good things to happen. The word patience carries the connotation of a hopeful expectation for good. The Holy Writ encourages devotees to possess their souls in patience. Throwing tantrums about the situation is inappropriate. Be proactive, take

action, and stop reacting to situations.

3. Pray. All religions encourage their followers to engage the Deity in times of trial. I found myself crying out to God Almighty for assistance on numerous occasions. I learned how to cooperate and receive Divine intervention (miracles) along the journey toward the desired change.

Don't give up! Your change **is** gonna come. "And it came to pass...." The Holy Writ

---

Trusting in the Lord
Jeremiah 17:5-8

There is a fine line between complacency and anxiety in situations. Trust in the Lord deepens my ability to recognize significant opportunities in life. A lack of trust can lead to distractions, disappointments and destruction. Verse 5 of Jeremiah 17 says, "Cursed is the one who trusts in man, who depends on flesh for his strength and whose heart turns away from the Lord."

Strive to make Proverbs 3:5-6 a reality! "Trust in the Lord with all your heart and lean not on your own understanding; in all your ways acknowledge him, and he will make your paths straight" (The Holy Writ).

~ Reflections ~

Epilogue

My journey has been very exciting. As a child I dreamed of traveling to places I read about in Ebony and Jet Magazines, the National Geographic Magazine, and the Holy Bible. Not many people from my neighborhood traveled in those days. Not many people from my neighborhood dreamed or imagined often. Or at the very least, not many people gave voice to the dreams or imaginations that resided in their hearts.

My childhood was filled with many opportunities to use my imagination or to dream dreams of what could be and what I could become. My mother taught me to believe in myself and in Jesus as God, to expect Divine intervention, and to exclude negative people and activities from my life. I did not always follow her directives. Her words were guardrails and caution signs for me as I grew older.

Like the Apostle Paul, I do not think I have arrived, but I am pressing to maintain the standard emblazoned on the tablet of my soul (Philippians 3:12, The Holy Writ). I will look to the Holy Writ to frame my perception; because perception is reality. I will continue to expect miracles, dream dreams, pray, and seek to develop a closer relationship with Jesus Christ. I have been involved with a few derelict individuals and in unprofitable activities. Now, I agree with Solomon, the wisest man in the world; fearing God and fulfilling the God-given destiny is to be the quest of all humans.

Take another look at Jesus, The Christ. Jesus provides the way for man to connect with God the creator of the Universe. Accepting Jesus' infallible sacrificial life offered in exchange for all the evil, wickedness, willful and deliberate violations of Divine Law and Principles is the only acceptable remedy to bridge the gap from God to humans (John 3:16, The Holy Writ). All humans have offended God. Ask for forgiveness and accept Jesus, The Christ. You are destined to be an Overcomer.

About the Author

Dr. Vivian Michele Jackson is veteran advocate for building strong families as the foundation supporting academic achievement. As an educator of special needs children, she taught in Ohio and Massachusetts Public School Systems. After marrying, she founded two Christian Day Schools serving families with children 2 years old through middle school.

A hallmark of the schools was the partnerships between the students, parents, and the school. Dr.

Jackson believes all children are capable of **learning in an environment characterized by quality instruction, supportive relationships, and personal responsibility.**

Promoting solid faith-based, social, and academic foundations, Dr. Jackson hosts conferences and workshops to help families develop solutions to build strong marriages, support one another to empower their children to dream, plan for the future, and develop partnerships between children and their parents. Dr. Jackson hosts family conferences, visits homes, and provides support services to students and their families.

Dr. Jackson, affectionately called "Dr. Vivian," believes that an enjoyable marriage continues after the birth of children when partners agree on solutions they can support and implement. Also known as *"The Marriage Doctor,"* she shares poignant information with couples to help them sustain a strong marital relationship.

http://www.the-marriage-doctor.com

Ordained to Christian Ministry in 1985, she has served as an Associate Pastor in with her husband. She is the First Lady of the International Communion of Evangelical Churches and Hope Christian Church. Dr. Vivian is an international conference speaker, seasoned with 35 years of Christian ministry. Ministry engagements include churches in the US, the United Kingdom, Kenya, Ghana, South Africa, Nigeria, Papua, New Guinea,

New Zealand, Germany, Honduras, and Toronto. She is a contributor to Gospel Today, Teachable Moments, and Living Wisely, online publications. She has published two booklets, *Radical Praise: It's Not Business as Usual* and *Where the Rubber Meets the Road: Surviving and Thriving in the Midst of Crisis*. She resides in the Metro-Washington, DC area, is married, and the mother of two adult children.

http://www.thehopeconnection.org;
http://www.the-marriage-doctor.com;
@MarriageDoctor2;
http://www.gospeltoday.com
http://www.teachablemoments.com
https://facebook.com/themarriagedoctor

If you enjoyed the book, send your comments to

drviv@the-marriage-doctor.com

or

Dr. Vivian M. Jackson
c/o Hope Christian Church
PO Box 505
College Park, MD 20741
https://www.thehopeconnetion.org

Books available at:
politics-prose.com
squareup.com/store/vivian-jackson

Get your copy...